Instant Pot Soups and Stews Recipe Book:

Healthy and Easy Instant Pot Pressure Cooker Cookbook.

By

Anna Moore

Copyright [Anna Moore]

All rights reserved. No part of this guide may be reproduced in any form without permission in writing from the publisher except in the case of brief quotations embodied in critical articles or reviews.

Hi!

Thank you for purchasing our book. Your support and trust in us are much appreciated. **Use this QR code** to get an electronic variant of this book as **a GIFT from us**! No more will cookbooks be ruined with unsightly splodges or splashes of cooking sauces, with our e-version.

How to use the book?

In each recipe you can see a QR code. After scanning this code, you will see a photo of the finished dish.

Why do we use QR codes in our books?

1) It is modern, innovative, and eco-friendly.

2) It saves book production costs, reduces energy, paint, and paper costs. This is our contribution to the care of the planet and the environment.

3) All this allows us to make the price of the book lower for buyers. Plus, you get not only the paperback, but also the electronic version of the book absolutely for free!

4) Thank you for contributing to the care of the environment with us!

Table of Contents

Introduction 7

Chapter 1 How to use the Instant Pot for making Soups and Stews 9

Chapter 2: Poultry Soups 10

    Perfect Chicken Noodle Soup 10

    Delicious Chicken Orzo Soup 11

    Creamy Salsa Chicken Soup 13

    Chicken Broccoli Soup 14

    Hearty Curried Chicken Soup 15

    Tasty Chicken Rice Soup 17

    Healthy Coconut Chicken Soup 18

    Chicken Tortilla Soup 19

    Chicken Avocado Soup 20

    Creamy Herb Chicken Stew 21

Chapter 3: Meat Soups 23

    Delicious Beef Vegetable Soup 23

    Hamburger Soup 24

    Flavourful Beef Barley Soup 25

    Beef Pasta Soup 26

    Beef Cabbage Soup 28

    Flavourful Beef Fajita Soup 29

    Steak Mushroom Soup 30

    Simple Pork Cabbage Soup 31

    Asian Style Beef Noodle Soup 32

    Lamb Stew 33

Chapter 4: Ham and Bacon Soups 35

Split Pea and Ham Soup 35
Ham Northern Bean Soup 36
Broccoli Bacon Cheese Soup 37
Creamy Cheesy Bacon Soup 39
Bacon Collard Stew 40

Chapter 5: Fish and Seafood Soups 42

Tasty Fish Soup 42
Shrimp Soup 43
Shrimp Tortellini Soup 44
Salmon Pasta Soup 45
Salmon Cream Soup 46
Salmon Corn Chowder 48
Haddock Veggie Chowder 49
Salmon Leek Soup 50
Flavourful Fish Stew 51
Seafood Stew 52

Chapter 6: Vegetable Soups 54

Delicious Squash Soup 54
Basil Tomato Soup 55
Creamy Carrot Soup 56
Mushroom Soup 57
Coconut Cauliflower Soup 59
Tasty Yellow Lentil Soup 60
Cabbage Leek Soup 61
Celery Sweet Onion Soup 62
Cream of Asparagus Soup 63
Healthy Vegetable Stew 64

Chapter 7: Bean Soups 66

Black Bean Soup 66
Veggie Bean Soup 67
Kidney Bean Broccoli Soup... 68
Beet Red Lentil Soup 69
Mixed Bean Stew.. 70
Conclusion 72

Introduction

A steaming bowl of soup is the ultimate wintertime comfort food. The fragrances and flavors of this comfort dish are a big part of its appeal, whether it's creamy or thick with vegetables. More than ever, though, stews and soups are an excellent way to showcase the best tastes of the season. Soup can be served as a starter, a main course, a side dish, or even for breakfast. What are the health benefits of soup? Vegetable, herb, spice, grain, and meat combinations are common in soup, which makes it a nutrient-dense dish.

An entire dinner can be served, as well as a nutritious side dish. It's not only simple to make and delicious, but it's also cost-effective. When it comes to weight loss, soup is a great option because it is both nourishing and filling. In addition to being easy to digest, soup provides a reliable source of energy for our bodies because of the combination of carbs, proteins, and other nutrients it contains. Because of its high nutrient content and accompanying energy increase, soup is the ideal healthy meal option. In vegetable soup, as well as other nutrients, vitamins A, C, D, and calcium are found.

According to a recent health study, tomato soup was shown to be the richest source of antioxidants and lycopene, which may help to reduce cancer risk. Lean protein is found in meat, beans, and fish in soups made up of these ingredients, whereas fiber is found in beans. The healthiest soup includes fresh vegetables, low-fat ingredients, and a minimum amount of salt. This book contains various types of delicious instant pot soup and stew recipes. The Instant Pot is one of the electric pressure cooker appliances. It is also called a "multi-cooker" and can do the jobs of a pressure cooker, rice cooker, slow cooker, steamer, and more. The Instant Pot is a new way of cooking a healthy and delicious meal at home. This book contains 50 healthy and delicious soup and stew recipes.

Chapter 1 How to use the Instant Pot for making Soups and Stews

How do you prepare soup or stew in the Instant Pot?

Instructions

1. To the Instant Pot, add the full soup mix, spice packet, and salt.
2. Stir in the water until combined.
3. Secure the lid and set the timer for 25 minutes on Manual, High Pressure. Then open the lid.
4. The soup should be done when it's the right consistency. Then, quickly release the pressure in line with the manufacturer's instructions.
5. Season with salt and pepper to taste.
6. Serve.

Chapter 2: Poultry Soups

Perfect Chicken Noodle Soup

Cook time: 30 minutes | Serves: 4 | Per Serving: Calories 302, Carbs 18.2g, Fat 14.4g, Protein 25g

Ingredients:

- Chicken breasts - 2, boneless
- Egg noodles - 1 cup
- Ground ginger - ½ tsp
- Chicken stock - 8 cups
- Bay leaf - 1
- Dried thyme - ½ tsp
- Peppercorns - 4
- Garlic cloves - 3, minced
- Carrots - 2, diced
- Onion - 1, diced
- Olive oil - 2 tbsp
- Pepper
- Salt

Directions:

1. Add olive oil and set the sauté mode to High. Sauté garlic, onion, and carrots for 3-4 minutes in the instant pot.
2. Stir in the remaining ingredients, except the noodles, until completely combined.
3. Cook for 10 minutes on High. Quickly relieve pressure and then open the lid. Using metal tongs, remove the chicken from the pot.
4. Set aside the chicken after shredding it with a fork. Select sauté mode on the instant pot and add the noodles. Cook for 10 minutes or until the egg noodles are tender. Reintroduce the shredded chicken to the pot and stir thoroughly.
5. Serve.

Delicious Chicken Orzo Soup

Cook time: 11 minutes | Serves: 6 | Per Serving: Calories 263, Carbs 26.3g, Fat 9.3g, Protein 18.8g

Ingredients:

- Chicken thighs - 2, skinless, boneless, and cut into chunks
- Fresh baby spinach - 2 cups
- Fresh lemon juice - 2 tbsp

- Orzo pasta - ½ cup, uncooked
- Lemon zest - ½ tsp
- Chicken stock - 5 cups
- Fresh rosemary -1 tsp, chopped
- Garlic cloves -2, minced
- Carrots - 1 cup, chopped
- Celery stalk -1, chopped
- Onion - 1, chopped
- Olive oil - 2 tbsp
- Black pepper - ¼ tsp
- Salt - ¼ tsp

Directions:

1. In an instant pot, add the olive oil and set the pot to sauté mode.
2. Add the onion to the pot and sauté for approximately 3 minutes, or until softened. Sauté garlic, carrots, and celery for one minute.
3. Stir in the chicken, pepper, rosemary, and salt. Stir in the stock, pasta, and lemon zest.
4. Cook for 8 minutes on High. Quickly relieve pressure and then open the lid. Stir in the spinach and lemon juice.
5. Serve.

Creamy Salsa Chicken Soup

Cook time: 30 minutes | Serves: 6 | Per Serving: Calories 300, Carbs 5.9g, Fat 19.2g, Protein 26.1g

Ingredients:

- Chicken breasts - 1 lb, skinless, boneless, and cut into chunks
- Fresh parsley - 2 tbsp, chopped
- Taco seasoning - 3 tsp
- Salsa - 1 ½ cups
- Cream cheese -8 oz, softened
- Chicken stock - 3 cups

Directions:

1. In the instant pot, combine the stock, taco seasoning, and salsa. Incorporate the chicken into the pot.
2. Cook on high pressure for 25 minutes, sealing the pot with the cover. Release pressure with the rapid release method and then carefully open the lid. Transfer the chicken to a serving dish.
3. Combine cream cheese and 1 cup of hot water in a bowl until thoroughly combined. Pour it into the instant pot. Stir thoroughly. Set sauté mode on the pot. Using a fork, shred the chicken.

4. Return the chicken to the pot and sauté the soup for 3-5 minutes.
5. Serve with a garnish of parsley.

Chicken Broccoli Soup

Cook time: 20 minutes | Serves: 8 | Per Serving: Calories 177, Carbs 4.9g, Fat 9.2g, Protein 18.2g

Ingredients:

- Chicken breasts - 1 lb, boneless
- Broccoli - 2 ½ cups, chopped
- Water - 1 cup
- Cream of chicken soup - 10 oz
- Garlic cloves - 3, minced
- Butter - 2 tbsp
- Paprika - ¼ tsp
- Black pepper - ¼ tsp
- Salt

Directions:

1. Set aside chicken that has been seasoned with paprika, pepper, and salt. Set the instant pot to sauté mode and add the butter.

2. Cook until the chicken is lightly browned on both sides. Transfer the chicken to a serving dish. Sauté the garlic in the pot for a few minutes. Stir in the water and chicken soup until completely combined.
3. Return the chicken and broccoli to the pot.
4. Cook for 10 minutes on high pressure with the lid sealed. Rather than opening the lid, relieve pressure using the fast release method.
5. Take the chicken out of the pot and shred it with a fork. Reintroduce the shredded chicken to the pot and stir thoroughly.
6. Serve.

Hearty Curried Chicken Soup

Cook time: 20 minutes | Serves: 6 | Per Serving: Calories 452, Carbs 9.4g, Fat 25.4g, Protein 46.6g

Ingredients:

- Chicken thighs - 2 lbs, skinless, boneless, and cut into chunks
- Fresh parsley - ¼ cup, chopped
- Coconut milk - 1 cup
- Spinach - 2 ½ cup, chopped
- Tomatoes - 1 cup, chopped

- Chicken stock - 4 cups
- Curry powder - 1 ½ tbsp
- Ginger paste - 1 tbsp
- Garlic - 2 tbsp, minced
- Large onion - 1, chopped
- Butter - 2 tbsp
- Black pepper - ¼ tsp
- Salt

Directions:

1. Set the instant pot to sauté mode and add the butter. Sauté the onion in the pot for 2 minutes.
2. Sauté the ginger paste and garlic for 1 minute. Stir in the curry powder, pepper, and salt. Stir in the chicken to coat with seasonings. Stir in the tomatoes and stock.
3. Cook for 5 minutes on High. Allow 10 minutes for the pressure to naturally relax before employing the rapid release procedure.
4. Carefully remove the cover. Set sauté mode on the pot. Cook in sauté mode until the coconut milk and spinach are incorporated, and the spinach has wilted. Serve with a garnish of parsley.

Tasty Chicken Rice Soup

Cook time: 13 minutes | Serves: 6 | Per Serving: Calories 321, Carbs 29.2g, Fat 7.9g, Protein 31.4g

Ingredients:

- Chicken thighs - 4, skinless and boneless
- Lemon zest - 1 tsp
- Dried parsley - 1/4 tbsp
- Thyme - 1/2 tsp
- Garlic powder - 1 tsp
- Celery stalk - 1, diced
- Onion - 1, chopped
- Carrots - 2, chopped
- Jasmine rice - 1 cup
- Fresh lemon juice - 2 tbsp
- Chicken stock - 6 cups
- Pepper
- Salt

Directions:

1. In the instant pot, combine all the ingredients and stir well. Cook for 13 minutes on High.

2. Open and take the chicken out of the pot and shred it with a fork. Reintroduce the shredded chicken to the pot and stir thoroughly.
3. Serve.

Healthy Coconut Chicken Soup

Cook time: 8 minutes | Serves: 6 | Per Serving: Calories 311, Carbs 19.1g, Fat 15.9g, Protein 26.2g

Ingredients:

- Chicken thighs - 1 lb, boneless and cut into chunks
- Swiss chard - 2 cups, chopped
- Can tomatoes - 10 oz
- Coconut milk - 1 cup
- Ginger - 1 oz
- Garlic cloves - 5
- Onion - 1, chopped
- Celery stalks - 2, chopped
- Turmeric powder - 1 tsp
- Chicken broth base - 1 tbsp

Directions:

1. In a food processor, combine the onion, half of the coconut milk, broth base, turmeric, tomatoes, ginger, and garlic.
2. Transfer the blended mixture, along with Swiss chard, celery, and chicken, to the instant pot and stir thoroughly.
3. Cook for 8 minutes on high pressure with the lid sealed.
4. Open and stir in the remaining coconut milk. Serve.

Chicken Tortilla Soup

Cook time: 20 minutes | Serves: 6 | Per Serving: Calories 395, Carbs 12.5g, Fat 23.1g, Protein 36.6g

Ingredients:

- Chicken breasts - 1 1/2 lbs, skinless and boneless
- Can tomatoes - 20 oz
- Cumin - 1 tsp
- Onion Powder - 1/2 tsp
- Garlic powder - 2 tsp
- Onion - 1, chopped
- Chipotle peppers in adobo sauce - 2
- Chicken stock - 14 oz
- Can coconut milk - 14 oz
- Dried oregano - 1 tsp

- Chili powder - 1 1/2 tsp
- Zucchinis - 2, chopped
- Paprika - 1 tsp
- Salt - 1 1/2 tsp

Directions:

1. Chicken should be seasoned with salt and placed in the instant pot. Combine all the remaining ingredients in the pot, except the coconut milk.
2. Cook for 20 minutes on high pressure with the lid sealed.
3. Open and take the chicken out of the pot and shred it with a fork. Reintroduce the shredded chicken and coconut milk to the pot.
4. Serve immediately after vigorously stirring.

Chicken Avocado Soup

Cook time: 10 minutes | Serves: 6 | Per Serving: Calories 234, Carbs 6g, Fat 6.8g, Protein 20.2g

Ingredients:

- Free-range chicken breast - 1 pound
- Garlic cloves - 2, minced

- Chicken broth - 1 quart
- Black pepper - 1 teaspoon
- Cumin - ¼ teaspoon
- Green onion stalks - 3, chopped
- Avocados - 2, sliced
- Salt - 1½ teaspoons
- Lime juice - 1 tablespoon
- Celery stalk - 1, diced

Directions:

1. Add everything in the instant pot except the avocado slices.
2. Cook on High for 10 minutes.
3. Serve with avocado slices.

Creamy Herb Chicken Stew

Cook time: 12 minutes | Serves: 6 | Per Serving: Calories 224, Carbs 17.5g, Fat 6g, Protein 24.1g

Ingredients:

- Chicken breasts - 1 lb, skinless and boneless
- Chicken stock - 3 cups
- Dried basil - ½ tsp

- Thyme - ½ tsp
- Ground sage - 1 tsp
- Garlic cloves -3, minced
- Onion - 1, diced
- Large celery stalks - 2, cut into chunks
- Carrots - 3, cut into chunks
- Potatoes - 2, peeled and diced
- Black pepper - ¼ tsp
- Kosher salt - 1 tsp

Directions:

1. In the instant pot, combine all the ingredients except the chicken and stir well.
2. Incorporate the chicken into the pot. Cook for 12 minutes on manual high pressure with the lid sealed. Allow 10 minutes for the pressure to naturally relax before employing the rapid release procedure.
3. Take the chicken out of the pot and shred it with a fork. Add 2 cups of stew mixture from the pot into the bowl.
4. Using an immersion blender, puree the stew ingredients until smooth. Stir well to incorporate the shredded chicken and mixed stew ingredients back into the pot.
5. Season with salt and pepper to taste. Serve.

Chapter 3: Meat Soups

Delicious Beef Vegetable Soup

Cook time: 23 minutes | Serves: 8 | Per Serving: Calories 226, Carbs 14.2g, Fat 7.9g, Protein 21.7g

Ingredients:

- Beef stew meat - 1 lb, cut into cubes
- Celery stalks - 2, chopped
- Carrots - 2, peeled and chopped
- Potatoes - 1 lb, peeled and cut into cube
- Water - 2 cups
- Chicken broth - 4 cups
- Dry red wine - ½ cup
- Garlic cloves - 3, minced
- Thyme - ½ tsp
- Tomato paste - 1 tbsp
- Onion - 1, chopped
- Mushrooms - 6 oz, sliced
- Olive oil - 2 tbsp

Directions:

1. Add 1 tablespoon of olive oil to the instant pot in sauté mode. Sauté the meat in the pot until it is brown on all sides. Place the meat in a bowl. The remaining oil should be added to the pot.
2. Sauté the onion and mushrooms for 5 minutes. Cook for 30 seconds before adding the garlic, thyme, and tomato paste. Combine broth, red wine, meat, celery, carrots, and potatoes in a large saucepan.
3. Stir thoroughly. Cook in soup mode for 17 minutes after sealing the pot with the cover. Open and serve after a good stir.

Cook time: 20 minutes | Serves: 8 | Per Serving: Calories 174, Carbs 10.6g, Fat 5.3g, Protein 20.5g

Ingredients:

- Ground beef - 1 lb
- Garlic - ½ tbsp, minced
- Chicken broth - 3 cups
- Can tomatoes - 14.5 oz, diced
- Frozen green beans - 1 cup
- Tomato paste - 1 ½ tbsp
- Potatoes - 1 cup, diced

- Celery stalks - 2, sliced
- Carrots - 2, peeled and sliced
- Onion - 1, chopped
- Olive oil - 2 tsp
- Pepper - ½ tsp
- Sea salt - 2 tsp

Directions:

1. In the instant pot, add the oil and set the sauté setting to high. Cook until the meat is browned.
2. Stir in the other ingredients until completely combined. Cook for 15 minutes on High and open.
3. Serve immediately after vigorously stirring.

Flavourful Beef Barley Soup

Cook time: 13 minutes | Serves: 8 | Per Serving: Calories 257, Carbs 26.5g, Fat 6.3g, Protein 26.5g

Ingredients:

- Beef stew meat - 1 lb, cut into cubes
- Mushrooms - 6 oz, quartered
- Garlic cloves - 3, minced
- Italian seasoning - 1 ½ tsp

- Onion - 1, diced
- Celery stalks - 2, chopped
- Carrots - 2, peeled and chopped
- Chicken broth - 4 cups
- Canned tomatoes - 14 oz, diced
- Dry pearl barley - 1 cup
- Olive oil - 1 tbsp
- Pepper - ¼ tsp
- Salt - ½ tsp

Directions:

1. In the instant pot, add the oil and set the sauté mode to High. Season the meat with pepper and salt and add it to the pot.
2. Cook for 3–4 minutes, or until the meat is lightly browned. Sauté mushrooms, garlic, onion, celery, and carrots for 2 minutes. Stir in the barley, broth, and tomatoes.
3. Cook for 8 minutes High.
4. Then open. Serve immediately after vigorously stirring.

Beef Pasta Soup

Cook time: 20 minutes | Serves: 4 | Per Serving: Calories 538, Carbs 54g, Fat 16.8g, Protein 44.5g

Ingredients:

- Lean ground beef - 1 lb
- Italian seasoning - 1 tbsp
- Pasta - 1 cup, uncooked
- Can kidney beans - 14 oz, rinsed and drained
- Carrots - 2 cups, chopped
- Bell pepper - 2 cups, diced
- Celery stalks - 2, chopped
- Tomato sauce - 1 cup
- Chicken stock - 3 cups
- Onion - 1, diced
- Garlic - 1 tbsp, minced
- Olive oil - 2 tbsp
- Black pepper - ¼ tsp
- Salt - ½ tsp

Directions:

1. Add oil and heat on Sauté. Add the garlic and onion and cook for 2 minutes. Cook until the meat is no longer pink.
2. Stir in the stock and tomato sauce. Combine bell peppers, carrots, celery, beans, and pasta in a large bowl. Stir thoroughly. Season with salt and pepper, and stir well.
3. Cook for 15 minutes on High. Allow 10 minutes for the pressure to naturally relax, then use the rapid release method to open the lid.
4. Serve immediately after vigorously stirring.

Beef Cabbage Soup

Cook time: 10 minutes | Serves: 6 | Per Serving: Calories 249, Carbs 9.2g, Fat 10.6g, Protein 28.6g

Ingredients:

- Ground beef - 1 lb.
- Garlic powder - 1 tsp
- Paprika - 1/4 tsp
- Canned tomatoes - 14 oz, diced
- Cabbage head - ½, diced
- Chicken broth - 5 cups
- Olive oil - 2 tbsp
- Onion - ½, sliced
- Garlic cloves - 2, minced
- Pepper - ¼ tsp
- Salt - 1 tsp

Directions:

1. Add oil to the pot and heat on Sauté. To the pot, add the onion and garlic and cook for 2 minutes.
2. Cook until the meat is no longer pink. Stir in the stock and other ingredients. Stir thoroughly.
3. Season with salt and pepper. Cook for 15 minutes on High.

4. Allow 10 minutes for the pressure to naturally relax, then use the rapid release method to open the lid. Serve immediately after vigorously stirring.

Flavourful Beef Fajita Soup

Cook time: 25 minutes | Serves: 8 | Per Serving: Calories 232, Carbs 23.3g, Fat 4.6g, Protein 24.5g

Ingredients:

- Beef stew meat - 1 lb, cut into cubes
- Ground cumin - 1 ½ tsp
- Onion - 1, sliced
- Bell pepper - 2, sliced
- Can tomatoes - 10 oz, diced
- Chicken broth - 14 oz
- Can black beans - 15 oz, rinsed and drained
- Can pinto beans - 15 oz, rinsed and drained
- Black pepper - ¼ tsp
- Salt - ½ tsp

Directions:

1. Add all ingredients into the instant pot and stir well.
2. Cook on High for 25 minutes. Serve.

Steak Mushroom Soup

Cook time: 15 minutes | Serves: 6 | Per Serving: Calories 212, Carbs 12g, Fat 4.4g, Protein 31g

Ingredients:

- Steak - 1 lb, diced
- Large bell pepper - 1, diced
- Large celery stalks - 2, diced
- Large carrots - 2, diced
- Water - 2 cups
- Oregano - 2 tbsp
- Garlic powder - 2 tbsp
- Mushrooms - 8 oz, sliced
- Chicken stock - 2 cups
- Tomatoes - 1 cup, crushed
- Bay leaf - 1
- Thyme - 1 tbsp
- Large onion - 1, diced
- Salt - 1 tbsp

Directions:

1. Select sauté mode on the instant pot. Sauté the meat in the pot until browned.

2. Cook until the onion, carrots, pepper, and celery are softened. Cook until the mushrooms are softened.
3. Stir in the other ingredients until completely combined.
4. Cook in soup mode for 15 minutes, sealing the vessel with the lid. Quickly remove the pressure, then open the lid and serve.

Simple Pork Cabbage Soup

Cook time: 30 minutes | Serves: 2 | Per Serving: Calories 288, Carbs 13.4g, Fat 11.7g, Protein 32.4g

Ingredients:

- Ground pork - 1/2 lb
- Cabbage - 1 1/2 cup, chopped
- Soy sauce - 1/2 tbsp
- Beef stock - 2 cup
- Carrot - 1 cup, peeled and shredded
- Small onion - 1, chopped
- Ground ginger - 1/2 tsp
- Olive oil - 1 tbsp
- Pepper
- Salt

Directions:

1. In the instant pot, add the oil and set the sauté setting to high. Sauté the beef in the pot for 3-4 minutes.
2. Stir in the other ingredients until completely combined. Cook on high pressure for 25 minutes, sealing the pot with the cover.
3. Quickly relieve pressure and then open the lid. Season with pepper and salt to taste. Serve.

Asian Style Beef Noodle Soup

Cook time: 25 minutes | Serves: 5 - 6 | Per Serving: Calories 496, Carbs 24.6g, Fat 11g, Protein 52.3g

Ingredients:

- Bone-in beef shank - 2½ pounds
- Tomatoes - 2, quartered
- Large onion - 1, quartered
- Garlic - 4 cloves, peeled
- Soy sauce - ⅓ cup
- Piece ginger - 1 inch, sliced
- Shaoxing wine - ¼ cup
- Beef broth or water - 3 cups
- Cinnamon sticks - 2
- Star anise - 3

- Fennel seed - ½ teaspoon
- Ground cumin - ½ teaspoon
- Ground cloves - ½ teaspoon
- Asian noodles - 1 pound, cooked
- Dried red chilies - 3–4, (optional)

Directions:

1. Add everything in the Instant Pot except the noodles.
2. Cook on 25 minutes on Manual.
3. Open the lid and mix in the cooked noodles. Mix and serve.

Lamb Stew

Cook time: 85 minutes | Serves: 8 | Per Serving: Calories 578, Carbs 7.6g, Fat 29.6g, Protein 67.7g

Ingredients:

- Lamb shoulder - 4 lbs, cut into chunks
- Beef stock - 4 cups
- Sour cream - 1 cup
- Mushrooms - 1/2 lbs, sliced
- Onion - 1, diced
- Garlic cloves - 2, minced

- Tomato puree - 1 cup
- Red wine vinegar - 1/2 cup
- Celery stalks - 2, diced
- Rosemary - 3 tbsps, chopped
- Olive oil - 1/4 cup
- Salt - 1 tsp

Directions:

1. In the instant pot, add the oil and set the sauté setting to high. Sauté celery, rosemary, onion, and garlic for 5 minutes.
2. Cook for 5 minutes before adding tomato puree, vinegar, pepper, and salt. Stir in the stock and meat well. Cook in meat/stew mode for 60 minutes.
3. Cook for an additional 15 minutes with the mushrooms on Saute.
4. Then toss with sour cream and serve.

Chapter 4: Ham and Bacon Soups

Split Pea and Ham Soup

Cook time: 40 minutes | Serves: 8 | Per Serving: Calories 203, Carbs 16g, Fat 7g, Protein 20g

Ingredients:

- Ham steak - 1 pound, cut into ½ inch chunks
- Olive oil - 1 tablespoon
- Bacon - 4 slices, chopped
- Medium onion - 1, chopped
- Garlic cloves - 3, minced
- Dried oregano - ½ tablespoon
- Thyme - 3 sprigs
- Bay leaves - 2
- Carrots - 2, peeled and cut into ½ inch chunks
- Chicken broth - 7 cups
- Dried split peas - 1 pound
- Salt and pepper to taste

Directions:

1. Select sauté mode in an Instant Pot. Heat oil in a skillet and add the bacon. Cook until the bacon is crisp, then add the onion and cook for 3 minutes, or until soft.
2. Combine the garlic, ham, carrots, oregano, thyme, and bay leaves in a medium bowl. Continue cooking for an additional 5 minutes. At this point, the Instant Pot's timer should be turned off; if not, press the cancel button.
3. After that, add the broth and peas. Combine all items thoroughly. Set the cover of the Instant Pot to seal and the valve to seal. Cook on High for 20 minutes.
4. It's time for the timer to start again. To get out of quick-release mode, press cancel and let the valve open naturally for 10 minutes.
5. When the pressure valve drops, gently open the lid and season with salt and pepper to taste.

Ham Northern Bean Soup

Cook time: 20 minutes | Serves: 4 | Per Serving: Calories 286, Carbs 39.4g, Fat 4.2g, Protein 23g

Ingredients:

- Ham - ½ pound, cubed
- Medium carrot - ½, chopped

- Medium onion - ½, chopped
- Garlic - 1½ cloves, minced
- Northern beans - ½ pound, soaked
- Olive oil - ½ tablespoon
- Medium tomato - ½, peeled and chopped
- Water - 1 cup
- Vegetable stock - 2 cups
- Dried mint - ½ teaspoon
- Thyme - ½ teaspoon
- Salt - 1 teaspoon
- Ground black pepper - ½ teaspoon
- Paprika - ½ teaspoon

Directions:

1. Press Sauté on the Instant Pot and add oil.
2. Add vegetables and cook for 5 minutes.
3. Add the remaining ingredients and mix.
4. Cover and cook for 15 minutes on Manual.
5. Open and serve.

Broccoli Bacon Cheese Soup

Cook time: 10 minutes | Serves: 6 | Per Serving: Calories 173, Carbs 26.1g, Fat 3.5g, Protein 11.2g

Ingredients:

- Bacon - 4 slices, chopped
- Small broccoli heads - 2, chopped
- Leek - 1, chopped
- Olive oil - 1 teaspoon
- Celery rib - 1, chopped
- Parmesan cheese - 6 tablespoons, grated
- Vegetable stock - 1 quart
- Spinach - 2 cups, chopped
- Basmati rice - ¼ cup
- Ground black pepper and salt to taste

Directions:

1. Add oil and heat on Sauté.
2. Add bacon on cook until crispy.
3. Add salt, black pepper, rice, spinach, celery, leek, and broccoli. Mix.
4. Cook
5. Cook on Manual for 6 minutes.
6. Open and sprinkle with Parmesan. Serve.

Creamy Cheesy Bacon Soup

Cook time: 15 minutes | Serves: 4 | Per Serving: Calories 346, Carbs 33.6g, Fat 19.2g, Protein 11.4g

Ingredients:

- Crisply cooked bacon - 3 slices, crumbled
- Potatoes - 3 cups, peeled and cubed
- Canned chicken broth - 1 (14-ounce)
- Butter - 1 tablespoon
- Onion - ¼ cup, chopped
- Dried parsley - 1 tablespoon
- Cornstarch - 1 tablespoon
- Water - 1 tablespoon
- Salt - ½ teaspoon
- Black pepper - ¼ teaspoon
- Cream cheese - 1½ ounces, cubed
- Frozen corn - ½ cup
- Cheddar cheese - ½ cup, shredded
- Half-and-half - 1 cup

Directions:

1. Mix cornstarch and water in a bowl.
2. Melt the butter on Sauté in the Instant Pot.
3. Add onion and cook for 5 minutes.

4. Add half of the broth, salt, parsley, and black pepper. Arrange the trivet.
5. Place the potatoes over the trivet.
6. Close the lid and cook on Manual for 4 minutes.
7. Open and add the cooked potatoes, cornstarch mix, and remaining ingredients.
8. Cook 5 minutes on Sauté.
9. Serve.

Bacon Collard Stew

Cook time: 25 minutes | Serves: 4 | Per Serving: Calories 324, Carbs 9.3g, Fat 2.1g, Protein 4g

Ingredients:

- Bacon - 2 cups, chopped
- Chicken stock - ½ cup
- Tomato paste - 3 tablespoons
- Collard greens - 1 pound, trimmed
- Pinch of ground black pepper and salt

Directions:

1. Cook bacon on Sauté in the Instant Pot for 5 minutes.
2. Add water, tomato paste, black pepper, salt, and collard greens. Mix.

3. Cook on Manual for 20 minutes. Open and serve.

Chapter 5: Fish and Seafood Soups

Tasty Fish Soup

Cook time: 13 minutes | Serves: 4 | Per Serving: Calories 213, Carbs 6g, Fat 6.6g, Protein 33.2g

Ingredients:

- Halibut - 1 lb, skinless, boneless, and chopped
- Ginger - 1 1/2 tbsp, minced
- Celery stalks - 2, chopped
- Carrot - 1, sliced
- Onion - 1, chopped
- Water - 1 cup
- Beef stock - 2 cups
- Olive oil - 1 tbsp
- Fresh parsley - 2 tbsp, chopped
- Pepper
- Salt

Directions:

1. In the instant pot, add the oil and set the sauté mode to High. Sauté the onion in the pot for 3-4 minutes.

2. Stir in the water, celery, carrot, ginger, and stock. Cook, covered, on high for 5 minutes. Quickly relieve pressure and then open the lid.
3. Cook the fish pieces in the pot for 4 minutes on manual low pressure. Release pressure with the rapid release method and then carefully open the lid.
4. Serve with a garnish of parsley.

Shrimp Soup

Cook time: 25 minutes | Serves: 6 | Per Serving: Calories 271, Carbs 4.9g, Fat 11.6g, Protein 35.6g

Ingredients:

- Shrimp - 2 lbs
- Dried rosemary - ½ tsp
- Chicken stock - 4 cups
- Butter - 2 tbsps
- Olive oil - 2 tbsps
- Fresh parsley - ¼ cup, chopped
- Tomato - 1, chopped
- Garlic cloves - 3, minced
- Broccoli - 1 cup, cut into florets
- Sea salt - 1 ½ tsps

Directions:

1. In the instant pot, add the oil and set the sauté setting to high. Sauté broccoli in the pot until lightly browned.
2. Sauté garlic for 1 minute. Cook for an additional 5-7 minutes. Stir in the shrimp, rosemary, and salt.
3. Combine the remaining ingredients in a large mixing bowl. Cook on High for 15 minutes.
4. Serve immediately and enjoy.

Shrimp Tortellini Soup

Cook time: 15 minutes | Serves: 4 | Per Serving: Calories 261, Carbs 21.4g, Fat 11.3g, Protein 14.8g

Ingredients:

- Raw shrimps - 8 ounces, peeled and deveined
- Olive oil - 2 tablespoons
- Tortellini - 1 cup
- Cherry tomatoes - 1 handful, halved
- Cloves garlic - 3, minced
- Basil leaves - ¼ cup, chopped
- Water - 1½ quarts
- Tomato paste - 1 tablespoon
- Spinach - 6 ounces, chopped

- Ground black pepper and salt to taste
- Red pepper flakes - ¼ teaspoon
- Smoked paprika - 1 teaspoon
- Italian seasoning - 1 teaspoon

Directions:

1. Add basil, garlic, tomato halves, pasta, tomato paste, and water to the Instant Pot.
2. Cook on Manual for 4 minutes.
3. Open the lid and transfer the mixture to a separate container.
4. Divide the pasta mix among serving plates.
5. Press Sauté and heat the oil.
6. Add Italian seasoning, salt, and shrimp. Cook for 5 minutes. Serve.

Salmon Pasta Soup

Cook time: 15 minutes | Serves: 4 | Per Serving: Calories 389, Carbs 22g, Fat 16.3g, Protein 27.6g

Ingredients:

- Boneless salmon - 1 pound, cut into small pieces
- Garlic - 2 cloves, minced

- Diced onion - ⅔ cup
- Baby spinach - 3 handfuls
- Strips bacon - 1–2, diced
- Mixed vegetables - 1¼ cups
- Tortellini - 10 ounces, uncooked
- Paprika - 1 teaspoon
- Quart chicken - 1 or vegetable broth
- Old Bay seasoning - 1 teaspoon (optional)

Directions:

1. Heat the oil on Sauté in the Instant Pot.
2. Add the garlic, bacon, and onions and cook for 3 minutes.
3. Add the vegetables, broth, seasoning, salmon pieces, and tortellini.
4. Cook on Manual for 6 minutes.
5. Open and mix in the spinach.
6. Press Sauté and cook until spinach wilts.
7. Serve.

Salmon Cream Soup

Cook time: 22 minutes | Serves: 4 | Per Serving: Calories 287, Carbs 40.6g, Fat 15.8g, Protein 47.4g

Ingredients:

- Salmon fillets - 1 pound
- Carrots - 1 cup, peeled and chopped
- Stalk celery - ½ cup, chopped
- Yellow onion - ½ cup, chopped
- Coconut oil - 1 tablespoon
- Cauliflower - 1 cup, chopped
- Chicken broth - 2 cups
- half-and-half - 1½ cups
- Ground black pepper and salt to taste
- Parsley - 2 tablespoons, chopped

Directions:

1. Add 1 cup water to the Instant Pot and place the trivet.
2. Place the salmon fillets over the trivet.
3. Close the lid and cook on Manual for 10 minutes
4. Open the lid and remove the salmon. Empty the pot.
5. Separate the salmon into small pieces. Set aside.
6. Press Sauté and heat the oil.
7. Add onions, carrots, and celery.
8. Cook for 5 minutes.
9. Add the cauliflower and broth. Mix and cook for 2 minutes on High.
10. Add back the salmon and serve.

Salmon Corn Chowder

Cook time: 10 minutes | Serves: 4 | Per Serving: Calories 428, Carbs 41.5g, Fat 21.3g, Protein 9.3g

Ingredients:

- Skinless salmon - 1 pound, cubed
- Garlic - 2 cloves, minced
- Melted butter - 2 tablespoons
- Small onion - 1, chopped
- Half-and-half cream - 2 cups
- Vegetable broth - 1 quart
- Stalks celery - 2, chopped
- Canned corn - 1 cup
- Yukon potato - 1, cubed

Directions:

1. Melt the butter in the Instant Pot on Sauté.
2. Add garlic and onions and cook for 3 minutes.
3. Add celery and cook for 2 minutes.
4. Add the potatoes, corn, fish, and broth. Mix.
5. Cook on Manual for 5 minutes.
6. Open the lid and add the half-and-half.
7. Serve.

Haddock Veggie Chowder

Cook time: 11 minutes | Serves: 4 | Per Serving: Calories 193, Carbs 21.4g, Fat 4.3g, Protein 17.3g

Ingredients:

- Haddock fillets - 1 pound
- Bacon - ¾ cup, chopped
- Carrot - 1, peeled and chopped
- Yellow onion - 1, peeled and chopped
- Celery ribs - 2, chopped
- Garlic - 2 cloves, peeled and chopped
- Butter - 2 tablespoons
- Potatoes - 3 cups, cubed
- Chicken stock - 1 quart
- Corn - 1 cup
- Ground white pepper and salt, to taste
- Potato starch - 1 tablespoon
- Heavy cream - 2 cups

Directions:

1. Heat butter on Sauté in the Instant Pot.
2. Add bacon and cook until crisp.
3. Add onion, celery, and garlic. Cook for 3 minutes.
4. Add stock, corn, potatoes, fish, salt, and pepper.

5. Cook for 5 minutes on Manual.
6. Open the lid and mix in potato starch and cream.
7. Cook on Soup for 3 minutes.
8. Open and serve.

Salmon Leek Soup

Cook time: 26 minutes | Serves: 4 | Per Serving: Calories 381, Carbs 12.3g, Fat 9g, Protein 53.4g

Ingredients:

- Salmon - 1 pound, cut into bite-sized pieces
- Garlic - 3 cloves, minced
- Chicken broth - 1½ quarts
- Coconut or avocado oil - 2 tablespoons
- Leeks - 4, washed, trimmed, and sliced
- Dried thyme - 2 teaspoons
- Coconut milk - 1¾ cups
- Black pepper and salt to taste

Directions:

1. Heat oil on Sauté.
2. Add leeks and garlic and cook for 3 minutes.

3. Mix in the broth and thyme. Simmer for 12 to 15 minutes.
4. Add the coconut milk and salmon.
5. Cook on High for 5 minutes.
6. Serve.

Flavourful Fish Stew

Cook time: 25 minutes | Serves: 6 | Per Serving: Calories 446, Carbs 8.7g, Fat 34.5g, Protein 28g

Ingredients:

- Cod - 1 ½ lb, skinless, boneless, and cut into pieces
- Fresh parsley - 1 tbsp, chopped
- Fresh lime juice - 1 tbsp
- Olive oil - 2 tbsp
- Cayenne - ¼ tsp
- Paprika - ½ tbsp
- Ground cumin - ½ tbsp
- Coconut oil - 6 oz
- Chicken broth - 8 oz
- Canned tomatoes - 14 oz, crushed
- Garlic cloves - 4, minced
- Bell pepper - 1, sliced

- Onion - 1, diced
- Black pepper - ¼ tsp
- Salt - ½ tsp

Directions:

1. In the instant pot, combine all the ingredients except the parsley, lime juice, and cod and whisk well. Cook on High for 10 minutes.
2. Add the cod. Then cook for 10 minutes in sauté mode, or until the stew has thickened. Cook, occasionally stirring, for 5 minutes, or until the fish is done.
3. Switch the instant pot off. Mix in the lime juice.
4. Serve with a garnish of parsley.

Seafood Stew

Cook time: 11 minutes | Serves: 6 | Per Serving: Calories 457, Carbs 26.7g, Fat 22.8g, Protein 38g

Ingredients:

- Shrimp - 1 lb, cleaned and deveined
- Fish - 1 1/2 lbs, cut into chunks
- Cilantro - 1/4 cup, chopped
- Littleneck clams - 10

- Chicken stock - 1 cup
- Garlic cloves - 2, minced
- Tomatoes - 1 1/2 cups, diced
- Bell pepper - 1, sliced
- Onion - 1, sliced
- Paprika - 1 1/2 tsp
- Bay leaf - 1
- Olive oil - 3 tbsp
- Sea salt

Directions:

1. Set the instant pot to sauté mode and add the olive oil. Stir in paprika and bay leaf for 30 seconds.
2. Combine the onion, cilantro, garlic, tomatoes, bell pepper, pepper, and salt in a medium mixing bowl. Stir thoroughly. Water and fish stock should be added. Stir in the other ingredients until completely combined. Cook for 10 minutes on High.
3. Serve immediately after vigorously stirring.

Chapter 6: Vegetable Soups

Delicious Squash Soup

Cook time: 8 minutes | Serves: 6 | Per Serving: Calories 88, Carbs 8.1g, Fat 7g, Protein 1.9g

Ingredients:

- Butternut squash - 6 cups, peeled and cubed
- Vegetable stock - 3 cups
- Onion - 1, chopped
- Butter - 2 tbsp
- Heavy cream - 1/4 cup
- Nutmeg - 1/8 tsp
- Cayenne pepper - 1/2 tsp
- Thyme - 2 tsp
- Pepper
- Salt

Directions:

1. Set the instant pot to sauté mode and add the butter. Sauté the onion in the pot for 3 minutes.
2. Combine the squash, nutmeg, cayenne pepper, thyme, stock, and salt in a medium bowl.

3. Stir thoroughly. Cook, covered, on high for 5 minutes. Allow for natural pressure release before opening the lid. Incorporate the thick cream.
4. Puree the soup until smooth with a hand blender. Season the soup with pepper and salt to taste. Serve.

Basil Tomato Soup

Cook time: 35 minutes | Serves: 6 | Per Serving: Calories 299, Carbs 13g, Fat 25.6g, Protein 7.8g

Ingredients:

- Canned tomatoes - 28 oz
- Romano cheese - 1/3 cup, grated
- Bay leaf - 1
- Fresh basil - 1/2 cup, chopped
- Fresh thyme sprig - 1
- Carrots - 2, diced
- Coconut milk - 1 3/4 cups
- Chicken stock - 3 1/2 cups
- Onion - 1 cup, diced
- Celery - 1 cup, diced
- Butter - 1 tbsp
- Olive oil - 2 tbsps

- Pepper
- Salt

Directions:

1. Set the instant pot to sauté mode and add the oil and butter. Sauté the celery, onion, and carrots for 5 minutes.
2. Stir in the other ingredients until completely combined. Cook for 30 minutes on manual high pressure with the lid sealed.
3. Quickly relieve pressure and then open the lid.
4. Puree the soup until smooth with a hand blender. Serve immediately after vigorously stirring.

Creamy Carrot Soup

Cook time: 10 minutes | Serves: 6 | Per Serving: Calories 82, Carbs 11g, Fat 5.3g, Protein 1g

Ingredients:

- Carrots - 8, peeled and cut into pieces
- Fresh lemon juice - 1/2
- Butter - 2 tbsps
- Garlic cloves - 2

- Onion - 1/2, chopped
- Ginger - 1/4 tsp
- Curry powder - 1 1/2 tsp
- Vegetable stock - 4 cups
- Salt - 1 tsp

Directions:

1. Set the instant pot to sauté mode and add the butter. Sauté the onion and garlic in the pot for 2 minutes.
2. Combine 1 cup of stock, curry powder, and carrots in a medium bowl. Stir thoroughly. Cook for 8 minutes on manual high pressure with the lid sealed.
3. Quickly relieve pressure and then open the lid. Add the remaining stock and puree the soup with an immersion blender until smooth. Stir in the lemon juice, ginger, and salt.
4. Serve.

Mushroom Soup

Cook time: 11 minutes | Serves: 2 | Per Serving: Calories 188, Carbs 10.9g, Fat 15.8g, Protein 4g

Ingredients:

- Mushrooms - 1 cup, chopped

- Chili powder - 1/4 tsp
- Chicken stock - 5 cups
- Fresh celery stalks - 2, chopped
- Garlic cloves - 2, crushed
- Onion - 1, chopped
- Garam masala - 1 1/2 tsp
- Olive oil - 2 tbsps
- Fresh lemon juice - 1 tsp
- Black pepper - 1/2 tsp
- Sea salt - 1 tsp

Directions:

1. In the instant pot, add the oil and set the sauté setting to high. Sauté the garlic and onion for 5 minutes.
2. Cook for a minute before adding the chili powder and garam masala. Combine the remaining ingredients in a large mixing bowl. Cook for 5 minutes on high pressure with the lid sealed.
3. Quickly relieve pressure and then open the lid. Using a hand blender, puree the soup until smooth. Serve.

Coconut Cauliflower Soup

Cook time: 15 minutes | Serves: 4 | Per Serving: Calories 263, Carbs 11g, Fat 8.2g, Protein 36.7g

Ingredients:

- Cauliflower florets - 2 cups
- Thyme - 1/8 tsp
- Curry powder - 1 1/3 tbsps
- Carrots - 2/3 cups, diced
- Onion - 1 cup, diced
- Olive oil - 1 1/3 tbsps
- Cashews - 2/3 cups, chopped
- Can coconut milk - 8 oz
- Vegetable broth - 2 2/3 cups
- Black pepper - 1/8 tsp
- Salt - 1/8 tsp

Directions:

1. In the instant pot, add the oil and set the sauté setting to high. Sauté carrots, onions, and cauliflower for 5 minutes.
2. Stir in the remaining ingredients, except the coconut milk and cashews. Cook for 10 minutes on manual high pressure with the lid sealed.

3. Allow for natural pressure release before opening the lid. Stir in the coconut milk well. Puree the soup until smooth and creamy.
4. Garnish with cashews and serve.

Tasty Yellow Lentil Soup

Cook time: 8 minutes | Serves: 4 | Per Serving: Calories 213, Carbs 31.7g, Fat 4.1g, Protein 12.9g

Ingredients:

- Split yellow lentils - 1 cup, rinsed
- Garlic cloves - 3, diced
- Tomato - 1/2, diced
- Onion - 1/2, diced
- Cumin seeds - 1 tsp
- Chili powder - 1/2 tsp
- Turmeric - 1/4 tsp
- Vegetable oil - 1 tbsp
- Water - 3 cups
- Salt - 1 tsp

Directions:

1. In the instant pot, add the oil and set the sauté setting to high. Allow the cumin seeds to crackle in the pot.
2. Sauté garlic and onion for 2 minutes. Sauté for 2 minutes before adding the chili powder, turmeric, tomatoes, and salt. Stir in the lentils and water until well combined.
3. Cook for 4 minutes on High.
4. Allow the pressure to naturally release for 5 minutes before employing the rapid release procedure.
5. Serve immediately after vigorously stirring.

Cabbage Leek Soup

Cook time: 20 minutes | Serves: 4 | Per Serving: Calories 173, Carbs 24.1g, Fat 8.3g, Protein 4.8g

Ingredients:

- Cabbage head - 1/2, chopped
- Garlic cloves - 2, minced
- Bell pepper - 1, diced
- Celery ribs - 3, diced
- Carrots - 2, diced
- Creole seasoning - 1 tsp
- Italian seasoning - 1 tsp
- Chicken stock - 4 cups

- Olive oil - 2 tbsp
- Leeks - 2, chopped
- Mixed salad greens - 2 cups
- Pepper
- Salt

Directions:

1. In the instant pot, add the oil and set the sauté setting to high.
2. Combine all the ingredients in the pot except the salad greens and mix well.
3. Cook in soup mode for 20 minutes, sealing the pot with the lid. Quickly relieve pressure and then open the lid. Stir in salad greens until they wilt. Serve.

Celery Sweet Onion Soup

Cook time: 30 minutes | Serves: 6 - 7 | Per Serving: Calories 186, Carbs 6.3g, Fat 14.6g, Protein 4.3g

Ingredients:

- Celery - 2 bunches, diced
- Vegetable broth - 1 quart
- Dill - 1 teaspoon

- Sweet yellow onions - 2, diced
- Coconut milk - 2 cups
- Sea salt - 2 pinches

Directions:

1. Add everything to the Instant Pot and cook on Soup for 30 minutes.
2. Open and blend with a hand blender. Serve.

Cream of Asparagus Soup

Cook time: 22 minutes | Serves: 4 | Per Serving: Calories 92, Carbs 18.3g, Fat 7.6g, Protein 6.4g

Ingredients:

- Trimmed green asparagus - 2 pounds, cut into medium pieces
- Yellow onion - 1, peeled and chopped
- Vegetable stock - 1½ quarts, (divided)
- Butter - 3 tablespoons
- Lemon juice - ¼ teaspoon
- Crème fraîche - ½ cup
- Ground black pepper and salt, to taste

Directions:

1. Melt the butter on Sauté in the Instant Pot.
2. Add salt, black pepper, and asparagus and cook for 5 minutes.
3. Add 1 ¼ quart of the stock and cook on Soup for 15 minutes.
4. Open and blend with a hand blender. Add the crème Fraiche, salt, pepper, lemon juice, and rest of the stock.
5. Press Sauté and simmer the mixture to boil. Serve.

Healthy Vegetable Stew

Cook time: 13 minutes | Serves: 4 | Per Serving: Calories 187, Carbs 39.3g, Fat 2.1g, Protein 5.4g

Ingredients:

- Potatoes - 1 1/2 lbs, peeled and cut into 1-inch pieces
- Large carrots - 2, peeled and sliced
- Flour - 1 tbsp
- Celery stalk - 1, sliced
- Leek - 1, sliced
- Olive oil - 1 tsp
- Vegetable stock - 2 cups
- Frozen peas - 1/2 cup
- Worcestershire sauce - 1/2 tsp
- Mushroom - 1/2 cup, diced

- Herb de Provence - 1/2 tsp
- Pepper - 1/4 tsp
- Salt - 1/4 tsp

Directions:

1. Set the instant pot to sauté mode and add the olive oil. Sauté mushrooms for 2 minutes.
2. Celery, potatoes, carrots, Worcestershire sauce, herbs, vegetable stock, pepper, and salt should all be added at this point. Stir thoroughly. Cook in stew mode for 10 minutes, sealing the pot with the lid.
3. Allow for natural pressure release before carefully opening the lid. In a small bowl, whisk together flour and 1 tablespoon of water. Stir well to incorporate the flour slurry and frozen peas into the saucepan.
4. Cook the stew for 1 minute on sauté mode. Serve.

Chapter 7: Bean Soups

Black Bean Soup

Cook time: 5 minutes | Serves: 4 | Per Serving: Calories 350, Carbs 68.9g, Fat 2.9g, Protein 19.1g

Ingredients:

- Can black beans - 4 cups
- Frozen corn - 2 cups
- Chili powder - 1 tsp
- Chicken stock - 4 cups
- Salsa - 16 oz
- Cumin - 1 tsp
- Salt - 1 tsp

Directions:

1. Add all the ingredients except for corn in the Instant Pot and mix well.
2. Cook on High for 5 minutes.
3. Add corn and serve.

Veggie Bean Soup

Cook time: 30 minutes | Serves: 6 | Per Serving: Calories 367, Carbs 68.2g, Fat 3.1g, Protein 22.5g

Ingredients:

- Dried white beans - 1 cup
- Dried pinto beans - 1 cup
- Dried kidney beans - 1 cup
- Bell pepper - 1, chopped
- Vegetable stock - 6 cups
- Garlic cloves - 3, minced
- Onion - 1, chopped
- Carrots - 3, chopped
- Celery stalks - 3, chopped
- Bay leaf - 1
- Salt

Directions:

1. Add all ingredients to the Instant Pot and mix well.
2. Cover and cook on Soup for 30 minutes. Serve.

Kidney Bean Broccoli Soup

Cook time: 6 minutes | Serves: 5 - 6 | Per Serving: Calories 162, Carbs 21.6g, Fat 4.1g, Protein 9.3g

Ingredients:

- Cabbage - 1 cup, shredded
- Oregano - 1 teaspoon
- Soy sauce - 1 tablespoon
- Onion powder - 1 teaspoon
- Carrots - 1 cup, chopped
- Green bell pepper - 1 cup, chopped
- Quinoa - ¼ cup
- Broccoli florets - 1 cup
- Kidney beans - ½ cup
- Vegetable oil - 1 tablespoon
- Garlic - 4 cloves, minced
- Vegetable broth - 1 quart
- Salt - ¼ teaspoon
- Lemon juice - 2 tablespoons
- Ground black pepper to taste
- Some basil leaves

Directions:

1. Press Sauté and add the oil.

2. Cook garlic for 1 minute.
3. Add the rest of the ingredients except for the pepper and basil.
4. Cover and cook on Manual for 5 minutes.
5. Season with basil and pepper. Serve.

Beet Red Lentil Soup

Cook time: 10 minutes | Serves: 4 | Per Serving: Calories 139, Carbs 16g, Fat 7.2g, Protein 4.3g

Ingredients:

- Carrots - 2, peeled and chopped
- Beets - 3, peeled and chopped
- Red onion - 1, peeled and chopped
- Bay leaves - 3
- Vegetable stock - 1½ quarts
- Fresh thyme - ½ teaspoon
- Sesame oil - 1 tablespoon
- Red lentils - 1 cup
- Dark miso paste - 3 tablespoons
- Parsley - 1½ tablespoons, chopped
- Ground black pepper and salt to taste

Directions:

1. Heat oil on Sauté.
2. Add onions and cook for 5 minutes.
3. Add the lentils, carrots, beets, thyme, bay leaves, stock, ground black pepper, and salt.
4. Cover and cook on Soup for 5 minutes.
5. Open and remove the bay leaf. Blend with a hand blender.
6. Mix in miso paste and season to taste. Garnish with parsley and serve.

Mixed Bean Stew

Cook time: 15 minutes | Serves: 3 - 4 | Per Serving: Calories 237, Carbs 36.3g, Fat 33.6g, Protein 12.4g

Ingredients:

- Olive oil - ½ tablespoon
- Medium white onion - ½, diced
- Medium carrot - ½, cubed
- Celery stick - ½, cubed
- Garlic - 3 cloves, diced finely
- Black beans - ¼ cup, soaked and rinsed
- Red beans - ¼ cup, soaked and rinsed
- White beans - ¼ cup, soaked and rinsed
- Cumin powder - ¾ teaspoon

- Salt - ¼ teaspoon
- Cinnamon powder - ⅛ teaspoon
- Bay leaf - 1
- Paprika powder - ½ teaspoon
- Chili powder or cayenne pepper - ⅛ teaspoon
- Canned tomatoes - ¼ cup, chopped
- Lemon juice - 2 tablespoons
- Vegetable stock - 2 cups

Directions:

1. Press Sauté on the Instate Pot and heat the oil.
2. Add garlic, celery, onions and cook for 4 minutes.
3. Add the remaining ingredients and cook on Manual for 10 minutes.
4. Serve.

Conclusion

The focus of this book is on utilizing an Instant Pot to create healthy and flavorful soups and stews. This book is for you if you can't get through the day without a warm cup of your favorite soup or stew, and you enjoy experimenting with new soup and stew recipes at home. The Instant Pot Cookbook presents you with a special variety of healthy soups and stews that can be made in a matter of minutes. They're an easy way to obtain your daily servings of veggies and herbs. A hearty cup of soup or stew is packed with nutrients that help you maintain a healthy weight and improve your overall well-being. Fiber, minerals, and antioxidants abound in these superfoods, which means they'll help you stay healthy and strong. They have a deep flavor and are easy to digest. Every aspect of your body will benefit from the many recipes in this book.

Printed in Great Britain
by Amazon